Dreamy Voices

Who's this dreaming up tunes?
It's 1155 and a nun called Hildegard is walking
through the gardens and stone buildings of the
monastery where she lives. Hildegard enjoys composing
music, writing poems, and is even inventing a secret
language. She studies the plants and flowers she can see, and
looks out over the soft green hills of the beautiful German
countryside. Words and melodies come to her when
she's daydreaming. She hears beautiful voices
blending together. "This tune seems to soar
up to the sky!" says Sammy.
Listen to the melody a few times.
Can you sing along?

Musical Tales

It's 1355 in the royal court in Mali, Africa. A great musician called Dugha is performing for the Mansa, or ruler, who sits on the throne. Dugha plays the balafon, an instrument made of pieces of rosewood strung together and hit with mallets. Other players strum on harps while acrobats twirl to the beat of a group of drummers. The musicians' songs praise great leaders and tell tales from history. "The balafon makes a magical sound," says Sammy. Across the continent of Africa, playing music runs in families. Musicians called jelis pass down songs from generation to generation.

Listen to the rhythm. Can you clap in time?

A Very Royal Sound

It's 1764 and young musician
Wolfgang Amadeus Mozart is traveling around
Europe with his sister Anna Maria. Their father,
Leopold has arranged for the brother and sister to play
concerts in grand palaces. Today, they are playing in Paris,
France. They like composing music, too, and eleven-year-old
Maria Anna helps Wolfgang write his melodies down.
He wrote his first piece when he was just five years old!
"Let's listen to one of Mozart's pieces for violin,
viola, and cello," says Pip.
"It's so bright and fresh—the sound of the violin
makes me feel very cheerful."
How does the sound of the violin's tune
make you feel?

PRESS to LISTEN

An Indian Raga

It's 1767 in Udaipur, India. Musicians, poets, and dancers are gathered in a beautiful palace on a lake. It's summer, and its marble pillars gleam in the sunlight. Fragrant gardens are blooming with jasmine flowers, palm trees, and vines. Water flows from the fountains in the many courtyards, and fish glide through ponds full of lotus flowers.

The musicians are playing a classical Indian Raga on the tanpura, flute, and drums. There are different tunes to play at different times of the day—this one is played in the morning. The Maharana Ari Singh listens, looking out at the magical scene around him. "This one reminds me of summer rain," says Sammy. *If you close your eyes, can you imagine being in the garden too?*

PRESS to LISTEN

All Together Now!

It's 1835 and 16-year-old Clara Schumann is performing with an orchestra in Leipzig, Germany. She's written all the music herself. See how her fingers glide across the piano keyboard. In these dramatic parts she can show off her skill. There are also slower, softer moments, where the audience can feel Clara's emotion. The conductor, Felix Mendelssohn, waves his baton so the orchestra can follow Clara. "This makes me feel as though I'm dreaming, says Pip."

Listen to the piano's solo. The orchestra will join in later.

PRESS
to LISTEN

A Sensational Story

It's 1875 and a wonderful performance is taking place at the Imperial Opera House in Vienna, Austria. Ballerinas, toreadors (bullfighters), and horseback riders come together on stage to put on a sensational show. They are performing an opera called Carmen, by Georges Bizet. An opera is a story told in music. This one is about the life and love of a gypsy girl called Carmen, who lives in the south of Spain. Like Carmen herself, the music is bold and exciting. "Listen to the energy of the orchestra!" Says Sammy.

"It makes me want to dance."

Listen out for the dramatic cymbals crashing at the end of each phrase.

PRESS to LISTEN

Sunrise in the Country

It's 1875 and Edvard Grieg is sitting a little red hut in his Garden in Norway. This is where he likes to come and write music. He's looking out on the lake, surrounded by mountains, and thinking how lovely it looks in the early morning light. He's just written a group, or suite, of pieces inspired by the play Peer Gynt, written by his friend Henrik Ibsen. "The flute sounds just like twinkling light on the lake," says Pip. "I think it sounds peaceful and calm, just like a morning breeze." *What does the flute sound like to you?*

PRESS to LISTEN

Toe-Tapping Ragtime

It's 1899 and pianist Scott Joplin is sitting
at the piano at his home in Missouri, USA. It's a
warm summer evening and his fingers fly over the piano.
He's playing so many rhythms at the same time that he sounds
like a whole band performing at once. Scott's well-known for
composing these catchy piano pieces, known as rags. He will go on
to write over 40 rags and become known as "The King of Ragtime".
"How can he play so fast?! It's so exciting," squeals Sammy.
Can you tap your fingers as fast as Scott Joplin
presses the keys?

PRESS
to LISTEN

Carnival Fever

It's 1911 and Carnival fever is sweeping Rio
de Janeiro, Brazil as musicians gather in the streets.
The musicians are playing music by Chiquinha Gonzaga, who
is leading the band. Her tango melody sounds out on guitar. It's
rhythm is perfect for dancing to. Everybody parades through
the streets of the city, dressed in their finest clothes.
People line the streets and watch from the windows.
"Come and join the street party," sings Sammy.
*Listen to the guitar. Can you hear the short,
spiky chords, and a melody on top?*

PRESS
to LISTEN

Bebop Jazz

Wow, what a band! It's 1945 in New York
and Pip is delighted to spot Charlie Parker and
his friends playing a concert in Harlem.
The quick style they are playing is known as Bebop Jazz.
Charlie on saxophone takes turns with the trumpet to play the
fast, energetic melody lines. "Look at Charlie's
fingers—they are moving so quickly!" says Sammy.

Can you have a go at making up the next piece of the music?

PRESS
to LISTEN

Pip and Sammy have heard so much on their musical adventure, but your journey doesn't have to end here!

As you've heard, there are so many different ways of making music, instruments and styles of playing to discover all over the world.

Our ancient ancestors made music hundreds of thousands of years ago, by using their voices to sing, shout and celebrate together. Over time, people crafted fine instruments. The earliest ones were made of shells, bones, parts of plants, and animal skins; later instruments were made of metal, and combinations of all sorts of materials.

Different kinds of music springs up in particular times and places. The churches of Hildegard's day were perfect for her calm, thoughtful melodies. The packed jazz clubs of New York in the 1940s were great for energetic tunes that soared over the sound of a crowd of people chatting and socialising.

Everyone can make music! It's such fun to learn. You don't have to own an instrument already—you can start by using your voice. For an accompaniment, pots, pans, and a wooden spoon make great drums, and you can make your own shaker from lentils, shells, or anything else that rattles, placed inside an empty container (like a milk carton). Many schools have instruments to play and even borrow. If you're lucky enough to own an instrument already, perhaps you could try out the different music styles you've seen in this book.
In the meantime, always keep an ear out and …

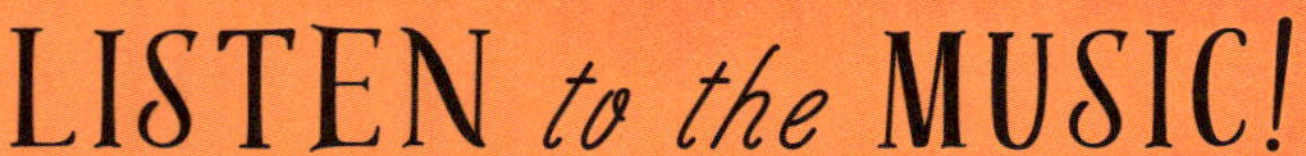

LISTEN *to the* MUSIC!

Brimming with creative inspiration, how-to projects, and useful information to enrich your everyday life, quarto.com is a favorite destination for those pursuing their interests and passions.

Listen to the Music © 2022 Quarto Publishing plc.
Illustrations © 2022 Caroline Bonne Müller. Text © Mary Richards

First Published in 2022 by Wide Eyed Editions, an imprint of The Quarto Group.
100 Cummings Center, Suite 265D, Beverly, MA 01915 USA.
T +1 978-282-9590 F +1 978-283-2742 www.Quarto.com

The rights of Mary Richards to be identified as the author of this work and Caroline Bonne Müller to be identified as the illustrator of this work have been asserted by them in accordance with the Copyright, Designs and Patents Act, 1988 (United Kingdom).

All rights reserved.

No part of this publication may be reproduced, stored in a retrieval system, or transmitted, in any form, or by any means, electrical, mechanical, photocopying, recording or otherwise without the prior written permission of the publisher or a licence permitting restricted copying.

Music licensed courtesy of Naxos Rights US Inc.
These clips have been edited for this book format.

A catalogue record for this book is available from the British Library.

ISBN 978-0-7112-7425-9
e-ISBN 978-0-7112-7424-2

The illustrations were created with mixed media.
Set in Brandon Grotesque and Cream.

Published by Georgia Amson Bradshaw
Commissioned and edited by Lucy Brownridge
Designed by Kate Haynes and Belinda Webster
Production by Chris Tucker

Manufactured in ShaoGuan, China SL062022
9 7 5 3 1 2 4 6 8